The Ethical Leader's Playbook

A New Era of Business Leadership

By

Colin Maxwell

Acknowledgment

I am grateful to Stephen R. Covey, John C. Maxwell, Peter F. Drucker, Daniel Goleman, Simon Sinek, Patrick Lencioni, and many others, whose ideas have guided this book. Their work continues to shape the values of modern leadership with wisdom and clarity. I also thank all mentors, colleagues, and readers, whose support and insights helped bring these lessons to life.

Author's Biography

Dr. Colin Maxwell is a well-known business consultant, author, and educator whose work focuses on modern leadership and ethical management. He holds a Ph.D. in Business Administration, is a Member of the Institute of Chartered Accountants (England and Wales), and a Life Member of the Institute of Professional Managers and Administrators (United Kingdom). His professional career combines deep academic knowledge with extensive real-world experience, helping leaders and organizations to grow with integrity and purpose.

Fluent in several languages, Dr. Maxwell has worked internationally in the areas of Business Consulting, Corporate Analysis, Management Information Systems, Training and Development, and the Valuation and Sale of Businesses. He believes that good theory supports sound practice, and that ongoing learning is vital for achieving lasting success.

He frequently conducts lectures, seminars, and interviews on topics such as Leadership, Business Ethics, Business Law, and Economics. His audiences include business owners, executives, professionals, and students from around the world. Known for his clear and engaging style, Dr. Maxwell encourages leaders to connect ethical values with effective management.

The Ethical Leader's Playbook continues his work on shaping responsible leadership in today's world. It follows his highly praised *Leadership: Pearls of Wisdom for the 21st Century* and earlier titles, including *Leadership, Ethics and Paradigm Shifts,* and *Leadership: 21st Century Food for Thought.*

Together, his books serve as a practical guide for leaders seeking to achieve success with integrity and a positive impact.

Table of Contents

Part 1

The Foundations of Modern Leadership

Chapter 1
The Compass of Purpose-Driven Leadership

Introduction

In an era of increasing ***volatility, uncertainty, complexity, and ambiguity (VUCA),*** leadership must extend beyond the traditional focus on short-term gains and profit margins. As <u>Stephen R. Covey</u> once wrote, *"Management is efficiency in climbing the ladder of success; leadership determines whether the ladder is leaning against the right wall."* The 21st-century leader must navigate a new landscape that is defined by purpose, ethical conduct, and a profound commitment to the broader community.

The goal is no longer just profit, but a more comprehensive measure of success, that includes the well-being of people and the health of the planet. This chapter explores how to develop a purpose-driven approach to leadership, linking it to established concepts of stakeholder engagement, the leader's personal legacy, and technological fluency.

The journey of leadership in this new paradigm is about building a legacy that resonates beyond the balance sheet—it is about fostering a culture where every team member is valued and empowered to contribute his or her unique skills and perspectives. The core of this new leadership is a profound sense of purpose that acts as a compass, guiding decisions and inspiring action. This is the leadership that inspires others to follow voluntarily and that creates lasting, positive change.

By integrating these principles, leaders can build organizations that are not only successful but also resilient, ethical, and deeply connected to the communities they serve.

Reflect on your own leadership style: *Is your ladder leaning against the right wall?*

Beyond Profit: The Triple Bottom Line of Modern Leadership (People, Planet, Purpose)

Traditional business models often prioritize the bottom line at the expense of other critical factors. However, a more sustainable and effective approach recognizes that true success is a result of balancing three key pillars: People, Planet, and Purpose, often referred to as the *"Triple Bottom Line."* For example, a shortsighted focus on drastic cost-cutting, such as mass layoffs, can be detrimental in the medium- and long run.

GOOD INTENTIONS ARE NOT ALWAYS TRUE INTENTIONS

Consider for instance, a manager who proudly announced the company's new "wellness and sustainability" initiative — *then handed everyone reusable water bottles emblazoned with the company logo.* The gesture looked great on social media until someone pointed out that the bottles were wrapped in three layers of plastic packaging, shipped overnight from overseas, and accompanied by a 15-page printed memo explaining how to "save paper."

The moment quickly turned into a quiet lesson on the difference between intention and consistency. The team laughed, not out of ridicule, but recognition — *they had all been there.* True purpose doesn't live in slogans or photo-ops; it shows up in the details. The most effective leaders are the ones who can smile at the contradiction, learn from it, and do better next time.

The same can be said about wastage of paper, when emphasizing the need to be cost-conscious and environment-friendly.

WASTAGE OF PAPER IN THE WORKPLACE

The modern leader understands that demonstrating a *"reasonable amount of concern for customers, employees, and other stakeholders"* is essential for a company's long-term performance and sustainability. This means fostering a culture where employees feel valued and are treated like a *"work family."* When employees are happy and feel respected, their stress levels are lower, and they are more likely to be creative, productive, and committed to the company's success. This approach to leadership builds a foundation of purpose, that aligns corporate goals with a positive impact on society.

Furthermore, purpose-driven leaders lead by example, rather than by mere words. They inspire employees and others to follow them voluntarily by creating an environment built on trust and shared values. This commitment to a higher purpose extends to the *"planet,"* where leaders are now expected to consider the environmental impact of their operations.

For instance, Patagonia's commitment to using sustainable materials and repairing their products, rather than encouraging new purchases, is a powerful example of a company leading with both purpose and a commitment to the planet.

As <u>Albert Schweitzer</u> wisely stated, *"Example is not the main thing in influencing others. It is the only thing."*

By integrating these principles, a leader ensures that the organization's success is not achieved at the expense of the environment.

The Stakeholder Revolution: A Leadership Mandate for Inclusive Success

The *"Stakeholder Revolution"* is a paradigm shift that demands leaders appreciate the values and feelings of *everyone* connected to the organization - not just shareholders! This includes employees, customers, suppliers, the community, and even government bodies. Success is no longer measured by the satisfaction of shareholders alone, but by the equitable treatment and engagement of all stakeholders. This involves ensuring *"workplace equality"* and a commitment to doing the right thing, even when it's difficult.

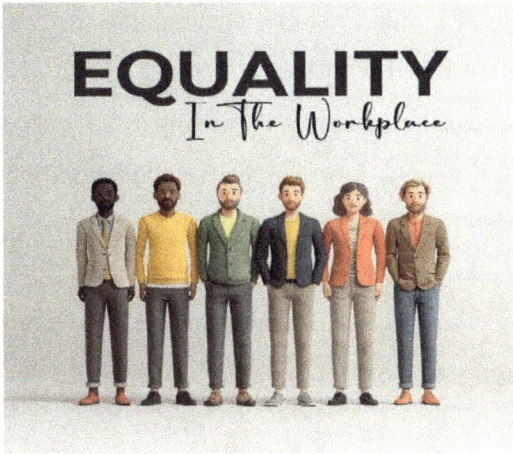

A leadership style that promotes inclusivity and treats employees with respect and dignity is crucial for a healthy and thriving organizational culture. The *"servant leadership"* model, which prioritizes the needs of others, can be a powerful tool in this regard. By listening to employees, encouraging their participation in decision-making, and respecting their ideas, a leader fosters a sense of belonging and empowers them to contribute their entrepreneurial skills.

This inclusive approach to leadership is essential for building a resilient and adaptable organization. By engaging with all stakeholders, a leader gains a more holistic understanding of the challenges and opportunities facing the company. This can lead to more innovative solutions, stronger community ties, and a more positive brand reputation.

For example, a leader might involve local community leaders in discussions about a new factory or might seek feedback from employees on a new company policy. This kind of open communication builds trust and ensures that the organization's decisions are aligned with the interests of all stakeholders. The stakeholder revolution is about moving from a *"shareholder-first"* mentality to a more inclusive, collaborative model of leadership that benefits everyone involved.

Identify your main stakeholders: *Are there any that you have neglected, and what steps can you take to engage them more effectively?*

Crafting Your Personal Leadership Legacy and Vision

A leader's personal vision and legacy are the compass that guides his or her journey. This requires more than just technical skills; it demands a strong character, authenticity, and a willingness to accept responsibility. A leader must be knowledgeable, confident, and willing to take calculated risks to achieve the company's vision. Leaders must also have the ability to persuade others to share in their vision and dreams, inspiring a collective commitment to a shared purpose.

As John C. Maxwell has noted, *"A leader is one who knows the way, goes the way, and shows the way."*

This kind of leader leaves a legacy not just of accomplishments, but of the people, who were inspired and uplifted. Promoting employees based on their character, attitude, and performance, rather than on non-relevant factors, is critical for building a strong and lasting legacy. The actions of leaders, rather than their words, will ultimately define their legacy and the impact that they have on the organization and on the community.

The development of a personal leadership legacy is a continuous process of self-reflection and growth. It's about understanding one's own values and aligning them with the mission of the organization. A leader's legacy is built on the decisions that he or she makes, the people mentored, and the culture that is created.

For instance, a leader like <u>Nelson Mandela</u> left a *"Legacy of Forgiveness and Reconciliation"* that continues to inspire global peacemaking efforts.

It is a tangible and intangible imprint left on the organization. A leader who is honest, trustworthy, and fair will leave a legacy of integrity. A leader who empowers his team and celebrates its successes will leave a legacy of empowerment.

Action to be Taken: *Write down three words you want people to use to describe your legacy. What actions will you take today to make those words a reality?*

The Digital Mandate: A Guide to Technological Leadership

In the modern business environment, leaders must be technologically savvy. The 21st century requires a growing need for *"Relevant, Accurate, and Timely Information (**RAT**)"* to be provided to motivated personnel, within a team environment. Leaders must be able to adapt to changes in technology and understand that technology, while a powerful tool for transmitting messages, does not replace the need for sound communication skills.

This includes communicating through advanced technologies, such as instant messaging and video conferencing. A successful leader in this new era will embrace technology as a means to improve performance and decision-making, while maintaining the human element of leadership and ensuring ethical practices.

BLOCKCHAIN TECHNOLOGY

Technological leadership is not just about using the latest software; it's about understanding how technology can be leveraged to achieve the organization's purpose. It's about using data to make informed decisions, automating routine tasks to free up time for creative problem-solving, and using digital platforms to connect with employees and other stakeholders in new and meaningful ways. However, this must be balanced with the understanding that technology is a tool— not a substitute for human connection. A leader must use technology to enhance, rather than replace, communication and relationship-building.

As a counterpoint, we must remember that *"technology is only a tool for transmitting messages; it does not replace sound communication skills."*

Leaders must also be mindful of the ethical implications of technology, ensuring that it is used responsibly and that data privacy is protected. The digital mandate for a modern leader is to be both a tech-savvy innovator and a compassionate, ethical leader. A point worth noting is that Artificial Intelligence **(AI),** while being respected, should be complemented by human intelligence, instead of being regarded as *"gospel!"*

Challenge for You: Evaluate your team's use of technology. Are you using it to empower them, or is it creating new barriers?

The Road Ahead

This chapter has provided a framework for a new kind of leadership: one that is built on a bedrock of purpose and ethical conduct. However, these are merely concepts until they are put into practice. The real test of a leader is not in having a vision, but in building relationships and fostering the trust required to make that vision a shared reality.

> **Leave yourself with this challenge as you move forward:** *How will you bridge the gap between your purpose and the people you lead?*

Think about it...

Chapter 2
Building Cultures of Trust: The Human Element of Leadership

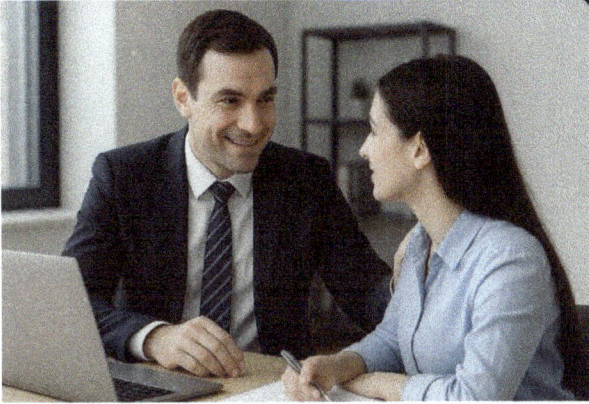

Introduction

In the complex world of modern business, while strategic vision provides direction, the true strength of any organization often lies in its human element. This includes trust, understanding, and genuine connections among people. These are the strong threads that make any organization truly last and grow. Beyond just plans and financial reports, leadership today is fundamentally about people. Therefore, it is important to create a place where everyone feels safe, valued, and genuinely able to be themselves at work.

As Patrick Lencioni, a renowned expert on team dynamics, states, *"Trust is the foundation of effective teamwork. Without it, fear and cynicism prevail."* This principle applies directly to how trust is built within teams.

Building this kind of culture means moving away from seeing employees merely as tools or *"disposable items,"* given that nobody is indispensable. Instead, employees should be seen as vital partners in reaching shared goals. It becomes clear that when diverse individuals feel safe to share their ideas, their combined intelligence contributes to improved performance through synergy.

In one department meeting, a well-meaning supervisor tried to "build trust" by encouraging open feedback. He began with, "Let's be honest — I can take it. Tell me anything."

The room stayed quiet until a new intern politely said, "Well, since you asked, maybe fewer 7 a.m. Monday meetings?" The supervisor nodded, scribbled a note, and replied with a smile, "Excellent suggestion — we'll move them to 6:30 a.m. to finish earlier."

The laughter that followed broke the ice — and revealed something valuable. Real trust isn't created by asking for feedback once; it's earned when leaders actually *listen* and adapt. The moment became legendary in the office — not because of the early meetings, but because the team finally felt safe enough to joke, speak, and be heard.

When trust grows, even early mornings feel a little lighter.

By putting people first, leaders can build bonds that go deeper than just work tasks. This creates a workplace where people stay loyal, come up with fresh ideas, and consistently deliver great results. This shift in thinking is crucial for navigating today's complex world, where human talent is increasingly recognized as the most valuable asset. This enables the formation of *a "work family."*

Ultimately, this chapter aims to help leaders create an environment where everyone feels they belong, understands their purpose, and can truly contribute. This isn't about quick fixes or superficial gestures. It demands a deep commitment to understanding and meeting the diverse needs and aspirations of a team. When these principles are applied, leaders can unlock immense creativity, resilience, and collective achievement, transforming their organizations into shining examples of ethical and impactful leadership.

Think about your team: *Do the members of the team truly trust one another? ...And more importantly, do they trust you?*

The Evolution of Human Experience Leadership

Leadership, as I have observed over many years, has undergone a significant transformation. It used to be about telling people what to do, much like a boss giving direct orders. The main goal was often just to get tasks done quickly and follow rules, treating workers almost like parts of a machine. However, in today's world, real, lasting success comes from how well people are doing and to what extent they feel that they are a part of the company.

This new way of leading, which I refer to as *"Human Experience Leadership,"* puts a strong focus on being kind, caring about people's feelings, and helping them grow fully. It recognizes that a happy and involved team is the true power behind a strong business.

This big change means employees are now seen not just as workers, but as unique individuals with their own dreams, challenges, and special skills. Leaders are now expected to be more like coaches and supporters, helping their people to perform at the highest level. This goes beyond simply dishing out tasks and related instructions. It means truly understanding and nurturing your team members.

It involves creating opportunities for them to keep learning and to grow both personally and professionally, and knowing that a good balance between work and life is key for them to stay productive and happy. It's about building a place where people feel seen, heard, and valued for who they are, not just for what they do at work!

Howard Schultz, former CEO of Starbucks, once remarked, *"We are not in the coffee business serving people, we are in the people business serving coffee."*

By putting the human experience first, leaders build a strong base of trust. This trust encourages open talks, lowers employee turnover, and creates a lively, strong team. This deeper connection builds loyalty and commitment, turning a group of individuals into a united and high-performing team that works together for shared success.

> **Your Next Step:** *Think about a recent talk you had with a team member. Did you only focus on the task? Or did you also care about their feelings and well-being? How can you add more kindness to your daily leadership?*

Psychological Safety: The Unseen Engine of High-Performance Leadership

At the very heart of a truly trusting culture is something called psychological safety. This is a shared belief among team members that it's safe to take risks with each other. When there's psychological safety, people feel comfortable speaking up, asking questions, admitting mistakes, and sharing different ideas without worrying about looking bad, being rejected, or getting into trouble. This isn't about being *"nice"* or avoiding disagreements. It's about creating a place where being honest and showing your weak spots are seen as good things. This leads to better decisions and constant improvement. *For example,* in a team that feels safe, someone might quickly say he or she made a mistake on a project, which allows the whole team to fix it together, instead of the mistake being swept under the rug until it causes a bigger problem.

On the flip side, if there's no psychological safety, new ideas will not be forthcoming, and problems will not be solved. In other words, important insights will be lost, and small issues will escalate, because no one will feel safe enough to point them out. This will create a dull and ineffective workplace, where creative solutions are stopped, and the team will not be able to easily handle new challenges. This will have an adverse impact on the team's performance and how quickly it can adapt to new challenges.

Leaders play a huge role in making and maintaining this level of safety. This means showing your own weak spots, truly asking for ideas (even if they are different from yours), reacting well when mistakes occur, and ensuring that everyone's voice is heard and respected.

As <u>Amy Edmondson</u>, who studies psychological safety, says, *"Psychological safety is not about being nice. It is about candor, about being direct, about being able to say, 'I messed up,' or 'I need help,' or 'I have a crazy idea.'"*

When psychological safety is present, teams are quicker, more creative, and more effective at handling tough problems. They become a strong force for desirable change within the organization.

Check Your Team: *Think about your team meetings. Are there people who rarely talk? What can you do to make it safer for them to share their thoughts?*

Unlocking Collective Genius: Diversity and Inclusion as a Leadership Strategy

The real *"collective genius"* of a company comes forth when diversity and inclusion are not just fancy words, but deep-seated ways of leading. Diversity takes into account the fact that people are unique—their backgrounds, experiences, ideas, skills, and who they are. Inclusion, as I see it, is the active work of ensuring that these unique people feel valued, respected, and that they belong. This allows them to perform at their highest level.

A diverse team without inclusion is like a band with all the instruments, but no one to make them play together; it just sounds bad and is unable to unleash its hidden potential. *For example*, a company that actively hires people from different walks of life and then offers special support programs to help them fit in demonstrates a real commitment to diversity, inclusion, and the building of a truly fair environment.

Leaders who want to unlock this collective genius know that if everyone is the same, things stop moving forward. When everyone thinks alike, important things are missed, and new ideas do not come to light. This can lead to blind spots and missed opportunities.

But when different ideas come together, it leads to more effective problem-solving, more new ideas, and a deeper understanding of different situations, which is of paramount importance in today's global market. This rich mix of thoughts and experiences is a powerful advantage that can lead to the desired level of growth and strength for the business.

Making inclusion happen takes real effort. It means challenging hidden biases, creating fair chances for everyone, and building a place where every voice is not just heard, but actively sought out and celebrated.

As <u>Vernā Myers</u> wisely puts it, *"Diversity is being invited to the party; inclusion is being asked to dance."*

By purposely building diverse teams and creating truly welcoming places, leaders tap into a wider range of ideas, experiences, and talents. This leads to better performance and creates a fairer workplace for everyone, making the organization stronger from the inside out.

Your Challenge: *Observe your team's diversity beyond numbers. Are you genuinely considering and valuing different perspectives? What steps can you take today to make your team more welcoming?*

The Motivation Matrix: Fostering Autonomy and Purpose through Leadership

Beyond the usual motivators like salary or bonuses, modern leadership understands the deep power of inner drive—the push that comes from inside each person.

<u>Daniel Pink,</u> who studies motivation, points out three key parts: *Autonomy (freedom), Mastery (getting better), and Purpose (a meaningful reason).*

Leaders who understand this *"Motivation Matrix"* empower their teams by giving them freedom, opportunities to grow, and a clear link to an important mission. For example, instead of watching every step of a project, a leader might give the team freedom on *how* it reaches its goal. This builds a stronger sense of ownership and responsibility, which naturally leads to higher-quality work and more job happiness.

- **Autonomy (Freedom):** This means giving employees control over their tasks, their time, who they work with, and how they do their work. It does not imply an absence of rules, but trusts and allows people to decide the best way to get things done. When people feel trusted to manage their own work, they are more involved and creative. This leads to a team that can change and adapt easily. This feeling of ownership is much stronger than any order from above.

- **Mastery (Getting Better):** This means giving people opportunities to keep learning and improving their skills. People naturally want to get better at things they care about and look for challenges that help them grow. Leaders help people achieve mastery by offering training, guidance, and challenging assignments that galvanize their hunger to excel. This creates a culture where everyone is always learning and becoming an expert. This investment in each person's growth directly makes the whole organization stronger.

- **Purpose (A Meaningful Reason):** This means connecting each person's work to a bigger, important cause. When employees understand *why* their work matters and how it helps the greater good (not just making money), their commitment and passion grow immensely. This fits perfectly with the purpose-driven leadership I talked about in Chapter 1. It turns daily tasks into meaningful contributions that truly matter to individuals.

As Stephen Covey said, *"Motivation is a fire from within. If someone else tries to light that fire under you, chances are it will burn very briefly."*

By cultivating autonomy, fostering mastery, and clearly showing the purpose, leaders don't just manage tasks—they light the inner fire of their people, thereby creating a team that is highly driven, self-starting, and performs at its best. This team is truly invested in the success of the whole organization.

Your Next Step: *Consider your team's freedom, growth opportunities, and sense of purpose. Where can you improve to better tap into what truly motivates them from within?*

Activities for Reflection and Action:

To begin applying the concepts discussed in this chapter and deepen your understanding of the human element in leadership, consider the following practical activities:

1. **Trust Audit:**

    - **Activity:** Take a moment to reflect on a recent decision or project within your team. On a scale of 1-10 (1 being low, 10 being high), how would you rate the level of trust among team members? How would you rate their trust in your leadership? Be honest with yourself.

    - **Reflection:** What specific actions or behaviors contributed to that trust level? Were there moments where trust was built or eroded? What were the barriers to higher trust? Identify one small, tangible action you could take this week to visibly build trust with one specific team member. This could be delegating a task you usually do yourself, asking for his or her unvarnished opinion, or simply following through on a small promise.

2. **"Tools vs. Partners" Assessment:**

    - **Activity:** Choose a current project or upcoming initiative. List three ways you are currently treating your team members as "tools" (e.g., simply assigning tasks without context, not seeking their input on *how* to achieve goals, focusing only on their output without considering their well-being). Then, list three specific ways you could treat them more like "partners" (e.g., involving them in the initial planning phase, asking for their creative solutions to problems, sharing the broader context and rationale behind decisions).

- **Action:** Implement at least one of the "partner" actions this week. After implementing, observe the difference in engagement, initiative, and the quality of the outcome. Note any changes in team morale or proactive problem-solving.

3. **Understanding Aspirations:**

- **Activity:** Pick three team members you interact with regularly. Can you articulate their individual professional aspirations (beyond their current job description)? Do you know what truly motivates them intrinsically (Autonomy, Mastery, Purpose)? What are their long-term career goals, or what skills are they eager to develop?

- **Action:** Schedule a brief, informal, one-on-one conversation with one of these team members this week. The goal is simply to listen and learn about their goals, challenges, and what truly excites them about their work or future. Make it clear this is not a performance review, but a genuine interest in their growth and well-being. Ask open-ended questions like, "What's one skill you're excited to learn?" or "What kind of work energizes you the most?"

4. **Observation of Belonging:**

- **Activity:** During your next team meeting or collaborative session, actively observe who speaks, who remains silent, and whose ideas seem to gain traction. Pay attention to body language and subtle cues. Are there any individuals who appear less engaged or connected, or whose contributions seem to be overlooked?

- **Reflection:** What might be contributing to this dynamic? Is it a lack of opportunity, fear of judgment, or feeling unheard? How could you, as a leader, create a more inclusive space for those quieter voices to contribute? This might involve explicitly asking for their input, creating smaller breakout groups, or ensuring structured turn-taking in discussions.

Your Path Forward: Turning Principles into Daily Practice

The heart of great leadership isn't found in lofty speeches or perfectly crafted strategies—it's in the daily choices that show people that they matter. Every conversation, every decision, every moment of listening presents an opportunity to strengthen trust, invite honesty, and remind your team that they are more than just their job titles.

When leaders choose to lead with empathy and vision, they don't just guide a team—they shape an environment where growth, resilience, and shared success naturally flourish.

> **So, as you step back into your role, ask yourself:** *How will I turn what I have learned into a living practice tomorrow? And how will my actions inspire my team to do the same?*

Carry that question with you, and let it guide how you show up for others on every single day...

Part 2

The Moral Core of Leadership

Chapter 3
The Art of Connection: A Masterclass in Leadership Communication

Introduction

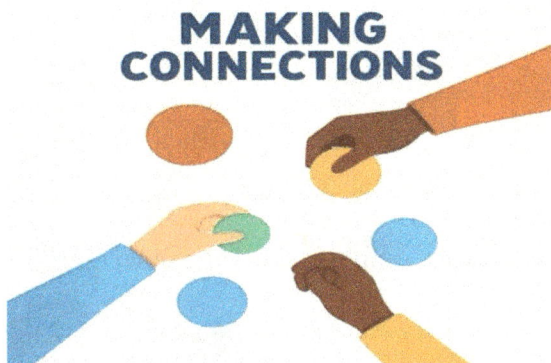

MAKING CONNECTIONS

In the modern workplace, leadership is no longer about issuing orders from behind a desk or delivering an occasional speech to rally the troops. It is about building genuine, two-way connections that inspire trust, loyalty, and shared purpose. Leaders are now expected to adapt to an environment where communication happens across many different channels—sometimes in person, often digitally, and almost always under the pressure of rapid change.

The leaders who thrive in this world are those who communicate in ways that make their people feel seen and valued. They listen as much as they speak. They explain decisions clearly. They invite discussion, instead of demanding agreement. They know that communication is not just a means to deliver instructions—

it is the lifeline that holds the team together, especially when challenges arise.

A true master of leadership communication knows that every message conveys not just content, but also intent, tone, and the potential to strengthen or weaken bonds.

George Bernard Shaw said, *"The single biggest problem in communication is the illusion that it has taken place."*

Whether a hallway chat, review, or virtual town hall, the goal is to connect, build trust, and progress.

This chapter explores four pillars of connection:

- ***Mastering digital body language*** *in a hybrid world.*

- ***Practicing radical transparency*** *by sharing truth with empathy.*

- ***Negotiating for value*** *so that all parties benefit and relationships grow stronger.*

- ***Treating trust as a form of currency*** *that must be earned, protected, and, when necessary, repaired.*

By the end of this chapter, you will see that great communication in leadership is not about being the most charismatic speaker—it is about being the most connected.

Mastering Digital Body Language: A New Frontier for Virtual Leadership

Not long ago, most of a leader's communication happened face-to-face. You could read someone's expressions, shake their hand, and sense their mood within seconds. Today, much of that has changed. We now interact through screens, emails, and messaging apps, where the small but important nonverbal cues we once relied on are easy to miss. This is where *"digital body language"* becomes critical.

Digital body language refers to the subtle signals we send through our online communication—the timing of our responses, the way we format messages, whether we keep our camera on, and even our choice of punctuation. Just as crossed arms can signal defensiveness in person, a curt, one-line email can suggest disinterest or irritation, even if that wasn't the intention.

Leaders who ignore these cues risk creating confusion or tension without realizing it. For example:

- *An urgent message left unanswered for hours can make a team member feel ignored or undervalued.*

- *Joining a video meeting with your camera off, while others are on, can suggest a lack of engagement.*

- *Writing "See me" in a chat without context can trigger unnecessary anxiety.*

To master digital body language, leaders need to be intentional:

- ***Acknowledge messages quickly***—*even if just to say, "Got it, I'll review this later."*

- ***Match your tone to the relationship***—*be warm and clear, rather than overly abrupt.*

- ***Show presence in virtual meetings***—*by looking into the camera when speaking, nodding to indicate you're listening, and avoiding visible multitasking.*

Considering cultural differences shaping interpretation is key. A brief, direct style may be valued in one culture, but seem cold in another. Awareness of these nuances enhances a leader's effectiveness in global communication.

As Erica Dhawan, author of *Digital Body Language, puts it, "In today's workplace, reading carefully is the new listening, and writing clearly is the new empathy."*

The words we choose and the way we send them can either bridge distances or widen them.

What's missing in most messages isn't grammar — it's tone!

A team leader once sent a quick message to her group chat after a long virtual meeting:

"We need to talk. Tomorrow, 9:00 a.m."

Within minutes, two employees privately apologized for things they hadn't even done; one asked if the company was downsizing, and another quietly updated his resume. By the next morning, half the team showed up on the call looking as if they had been summoned for judgment.

The leader's intent had been simple — to discuss an upcoming project launch — but her tone, stripped of facial cues and warmth, had taken on a life of its own. The meeting turned into an unplanned communication workshop, proving once again that digital body language isn't just about what we say, but *how* we type, pause, and punctuate.

From that day on, her messages always ended with a smile emoji or a few extra words of context — not to decorate the sentence, but to restore calm. Sometimes, the smallest symbols rebuild the biggest bridges!

Context, warmth, and a few extra words — the true emojis of leadership.

Ask your employees: *How do they interpret your messages and virtual presence? Do they see you as approachable or distant? What one small change—like a warmer greeting, quicker acknowledgment, or more focused video—could make your digital communication feel more human?*

Radical Transparency: The Power of Honest and Empathetic Leadership

Transparency builds trust faster than almost any other leadership behavior—but only when coupled with empathy. Radical transparency means going beyond the surface-level updates and being willing to share the reality of what's happening, even if the news is uncomfortable. It's about trusting your team enough to give them the whole picture, while also caring deeply about how that truth will affect them.

Some leaders fear that being too transparent will create panic or doubt. But in most cases, silence and half-truths do far more harm. Without real information, people will fill the gap with speculation—and speculation almost always paints a darker picture.

Radical transparency is not dumping raw data on your team without explanation. It is giving context, explaining the *"why,"* and inviting people into the problem-solving process. For instance:

- **Instead of saying,** *"We have to make cuts,"* **you might explain**, *"Our operating costs have risen 20% over the past year, while revenue has stayed flat. To stay competitive, we need to reduce expenses in a way that keeps our mission strong. Here's what we're considering, and here's where we want your input."*

This approach respects people's intelligence and treats them as partners, not just employees waiting for orders. It also builds loyalty because people feel included, even when the circumstances are tough.

Radical transparency also helps correct mistakes faster. When leaders are open about challenges, more minds can contribute to solutions.

As <u>Patrick Lencioni</u> reminds us, *"When there is trust, conflict becomes nothing but the pursuit of truth."*

Sharing reality openly makes space for healthy conflict that leads to better decisions.

Reflect on a time you concealed information from your team: Did it improve the outcome or cause confusion? How might honesty and compassion from the start have changed things?

Negotiating for Value: A Leadership Approach to Win-Win Scenarios

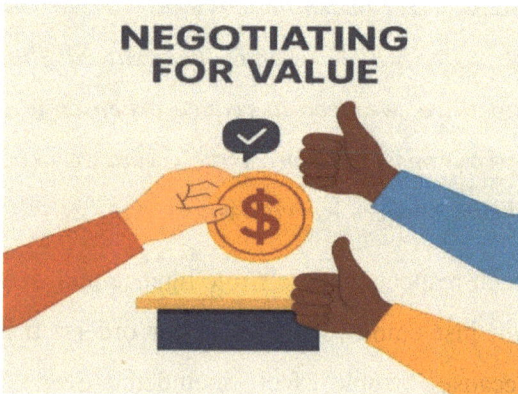

In leadership, negotiation happens far more often than we realize. It's not just about contracts with suppliers or deals with partners. Every time you balance priorities between departments, adjust timelines with your team, or decide on resource allocation, you are negotiating. The key difference between an average leader and a great, one is the ability to negotiate in a way that strengthens relationships, instead of straining them.

Too often, negotiations are approached like battles—one side wins, while the other side loses. But effective leadership negotiation works from a different mindset: both sides should walk away feeling that they have gained something of value. This is what is often called the *"win-win"* approach. In practice, the latter requires more listening than talking.

Leaders who negotiate for value begin by asking genuine questions:

- *What matters most to the other side?*

- *What challenges are they facing that we might help solve?*

- *Where are our goals aligned, and where can we be flexible?*

By focusing on these questions first, leaders uncover opportunities that might otherwise be missed.

For example, *a supplier* asking for higher prices may be open to locking in a longer-term contract for stability, which benefits both sides. A team member requesting more flexible hours might also agree to take on responsibilities that better fit his or her peak productivity times.

The power of this approach is that it converts the conversation from a tug-of-war into a joint problem-solving session.

As <u>Stephen Covey</u> famously wrote, *"Seek first to understand, then to be understood."*

When people feel heard and respected, they are far more likely to compromise.

Negotiating for value also requires considering the long-term impact of your decisions. Pushing for the absolute best deal for yourself in the short term can erode goodwill, making future collaboration less likely. In leadership, every negotiation is an investment in trust.

Challenge yourself in your next negotiation—whether with a colleague, a client, or your team: *What would it take for this to be a win for everyone involved, and are you prepared to truly listen to the answer?*

The Currency of Trust: How Leadership Can Build, Keep, and Repair It

Trust is the invisible currency that fuels every successful organization. When it is present, people take risks, share ideas, and commit fully to their work. When it is absent, even the most detailed strategies fall flat. The challenge for leaders is that trust is slow to earn and quick to lose.

Building trust begins with consistency between words and actions. If you promise to follow up on an idea, do it. If you commit to supporting your team in a decision, stand by them when it counts. Reliability is the foundation. Without it, trust will never take root.

Honesty is the next layer. This does not mean saying everything without filter, but it does mean telling the truth, even when it is uncomfortable. People would rather hear, *"We're facing a challenge, and here's how we're addressing it,"* than be left in the dark.

And finally, trust is built on genuine care. When leaders take the time to ask about a team member's challenges, support his or her growth, and celebrate the latter person's wins, it sends the following message: *"You matter."*

"Trust is built when someone is vulnerable and not taken advantage of." — Bob Vanourek

But what happens when trust is damaged?

Maybe a commitment was broken, or a decision was made without consultation.

The repair process isn't instant—it is a series of deliberate actions:

1. *Acknowledge* the breach directly.

2. *Apologize* sincerely without making excuses.

3. *Act* consistently over time to prove reliability.

A leader who admits, *"I know I didn't follow through on my promise, and I understand that may have hurt your confidence in me. Here's what I'm doing to make it right,"* opens the door for trust to rebuild. Without acknowledgment, that door often stays shut.

Ask your team: *To share one thing you could do to strengthen their trust in your leadership. Listen without defensiveness, and act on at least one of those suggestions this week.*

Activities for Reflection and Action:

To help you apply the principles from this chapter, here are practical steps and reflection prompts you can take into your leadership practice right away:

1. **Digital Presence Check**

    - **Activity**: Review your last five digital interactions—emails, messages, or video calls. How might your tone, speed of response, or level of presence have been interpreted?
    - **Action**: Pick one specific improvement, such as adding more context in messages or maintaining stronger video engagement, and apply it consistently this week.

2. **Transparency Test**

    - **Activity**: Identify one current challenge in your team or organization that you have been holding back on sharing.
    - **Action**: Prepare a short, empathetic explanation that provides context and invites input. Share it in your next team meeting and note the response.

3. **Value-Based Negotiation**

    - **Activity**: Think of an upcoming negotiation— formal or informal. List what you want from it, then list what the other party might want.
    - **Action**: In the conversation, focus first on understanding the other party's priorities. Look for

a solution that benefits both sides, even if it was not part of the original plan.

4. **Trust Audit**

- **Activity**: On a scale of 1–10, rate the current trust level between you and your team.

- **Action**: Ask three team members privately what you could do to raise that score. Choose one suggestion and act on it this week.

Maintaining the Connection: Making Communication Your Leadership Superpower

The art of connection is the heartbeat of effective leadership. It's in the quick acknowledgment that makes someone feel heard, the transparent conversation that clears away doubt, the fair negotiation that leaves both sides satisfied, and the daily actions that build a bank of trust over time.

Simon Sinek's quote, *"Leadership is not about being in charge. It is about taking care of those in your charge."*

In this context, *"servant leadership"* is of paramount importance.

Leaders who communicate well don't just manage information—they shape culture. They make people feel safe to speak up, confident in their direction, and proud to contribute. These connections are built, not in grand gestures, but in the thousands of small moments, when a leader chooses clarity, empathy, and integrity.

As you approach your next interaction—whether a casual chat, tense meeting, or tough decision—pause and ask yourself: *Am I just transmitting information, or am I building a connection that will last?*

Chapter 4
The Ethical Backbone: Forging a Resilient Moral Leadership Core

Introduction

Every leader carries an invisible weight: the responsibility of trust. Teams look up not only for direction, but also for assurance that decisions are made with fairness, respect, and integrity. Leadership without ethics is like a bridge without pillars; it may stand for a while, but eventually, it collapses under pressure.

The modern world doesn't make this easy. New technologies, global competition, shifting regulations, and diverse cultures create dilemmas where the *"right"* path is not always obvious. Yet, it is precisely in these gray areas that leaders reveal their true character.

As former US Supreme Court Justice, Potter Stewart once remarked, *"Ethics is knowing the difference between what you have a right to do and what is right to do."*

This chapter focuses on what it means to forge a resilient moral leadership core. We'll explore:

- *How leaders move from **gray zones** of uncertainty to clear green lights of principled action.*

- *Why integrity is not just moral, but also practical and profitable.*

- *How to **architect an ethical culture** that lives beyond policies.*

- *And how **emotional intelligence** works as a moral compass in difficult times.*

At the end, you'll see that ethical leadership is not about perfection—it's about consistency, courage, and building a backbone that is strong enough to hold the weight of trust.

Stop for a second and think: When was the last time you felt truly proud of a decision—not because it was popular, but because it was right?

From Gray Zones to Green Lights: A Modern Framework for Ethical Leadership

Ethical leadership today is less about avoiding clear-cut wrongs and more about navigating the fog of *"in-between."* Take the example of a tech company faced with collecting user data. Should they gather as much as legally possible, or set stricter self-limits out of respect for privacy? One option maximizes short-term revenue. The other option builds long-term trust.

Gray zones like this demand courage. Without a framework, leaders may freeze—or worse, make impulsive choices that they regret later on.

Here's a four-step framework that many effective leaders use to move from uncertainty to clarity:

1. **Clarify the Stakeholders** – *Ask: Who gains and who loses with this decision? Ethics expands the circle beyond shareholders to include employees, customers, suppliers, communities, the government, and even the environment.*

2. **Check the Values** – *Ask: Does this action reflect or betray our core values? As Peter Drucker once put it, "Management is doing things right; leadership is doing the right things."*

3. **Seek Transparency** – *Ask: Would I be comfortable if this decision were published tomorrow on the front page of The New York Times? If the answer is no, something is off.*

4. **Choose the Lasting Good** – *Ask: Which path may cost more today, but pays off in reputation, trust, and resilience tomorrow?*

This framework is not about avoiding risk—it's about aligning choices with principle.

As <u>Warren Buffett </u>wisely said, *"It takes 20 years to build a reputation and five minutes to ruin it."*

Consider **Starbucks**. In 2018, after an incident of racial profiling in one of its stores, the company closed more than *8,000 locations* for an afternoon of anti-bias training. Costly? Yes! But the decision demonstrated values in action.

Action to be taken: Pick one decision you're wrestling with this week. Run it through the four steps. Notice if the answer changes once you shift from "short-term convenience" to "long-term rightness."

The Integrity Advantage: Why Good Ethics is Great Leadership

Many people assume ethics and business results are at odds, as if integrity slows progress. In reality, integrity is one of the strongest competitive advantages that a leader can have.

Trust is the currency of modern leadership. Teams that trust their leaders put forth a greater effort. Customers that trust a company stay loyal even when competitors offer discounts. Investors that trust an organization, weather downturns with patience. Integrity pays—both morally and materially.

Take **Johnson & Johnson's** handling of the *Tylenol* crisis. In the early 1980s, after tampering led to several deaths, the company could have minimized the incident. Instead, it ordered a nationwide recall, redesigned packaging, and communicated with full transparency. In the short term, the company lost millions. In the long term, it gained unmatched trust. Today, the case is still studied as an example of *"the integrity advantage."*

On the flip side, history is filled with cautionary tales of leaders who traded ethics for shortcuts. Enron collapsed under the weight of lies. Volkswagen paid billions for emissions cheating. The Wells Fargo's fake accounts scandal led to broken trust with millions of customers.

Stephen R. Covey once noted, *"Trust is the glue of life. It's the most essential ingredient in effective communication. It's the foundational principle that holds all relationships."*

Integrity is not about avoiding mistakes—it's about handling them honestly. A leader who admits fault, apologizes sincerely, and takes corrective action will often emerge stronger than one who tries to cover it up.

Reflection for you: If someone asked your team to describe your leadership in three words, would "trustworthy" be one of them? If not, what needs to change?

Architecting an Ethical Culture: Leadership from Code of Conduct to Daily Conduct

THE CODE OF CONDUCT

BE RESPECTFUL   BE HONEST   BE RESPONSIBLE   BE FAIR

A company's ethical culture is not written on posters—it is lived in hallways, meetings, and daily choices. An organization may have the most polished *"code of conduct,"* but if leaders focus on rewarding results at all costs, the real culture is clear.

Friendly teamwork or more? In today's workplace, perception can turn a photo into a policy review.

Sometimes, corporate ethics aren't tested in boardrooms — *they're tested in breakrooms.* It's the small, everyday moments that reveal how people interpret professionalism. Take two employees sharing a brief photo after a project win: *one gesture too close, one glance misread, and suddenly, a light exchange can spiral into whispered opinions or even a formal complaint.*

In such moments, the question isn't who's guilty—it's whether both individuals understood the fine balance between friendliness and too much friendliness, i.e., flirtation. The modern workplace operates on more than policy; it runs on awareness. What feels harmless to one person may feel intrusive to another, and that gap is where misunderstandings grow.

Leaders must remind teams that respect isn't about avoiding connection — *it's about clarity, consent, and context.* A culture of awareness prevents minor incidents from becoming major lessons.

Professional confidence can either inspire others or invite scrutiny, depending on how it is presented.

Building an ethical culture requires moving from statements to systems:

1. **Lead by Example** – *Employees watch what leaders do, rather than what they merely say. If leaders cut corners, even once, they silently give permission for others to do the same.*

2. **Reward Integrity** – *Promotions should highlight not just "what" people achieved, but "how." Did they treat colleagues fairly? Did they respect customers? Did they uphold values under pressure?*

3. **Encourage Speaking Up** – *Silence is where misconduct grows. Create safe channels—anonymous hotlines, open-*

door policies, whistleblower protections—where employees feel empowered to raise concerns.

4. ***Normalize Ethical Language*** – *In meetings, ask: "Is this aligned with our values?" When leaders make this question part of routine conversation, ethics becomes muscle memory.*

As <u>Albert Schweitzer</u> once observed, *"Example is not the main thing in influencing others. It is the only thing."*

Patagonia offers a prime example. The company's mission is clear: *"We're in business to save our home planet."* This isn't just a slogan—it's lived in product design, supply chain choices, and even in encouraging customers to repair, rather than replace clothing. Ethics is built into the business model itself.

> **Challenge for you:** Take a "culture walk." Step into your own workplace, as if you were a new hire. In the first week, what would be more obvious—policies on a wall, or behaviors that confirm them?

Emotional Intelligence as a Moral Compass for Leadership

When leaders face ethical dilemmas, logic and rules may point in several directions. What often tips the balance is emotional intelligence—the ability to understand emotions, empathize with others, and act with balanced self-awareness.

Emotional intelligence (EI) helps leaders recognize when a decision may be *"technically correct,"* but morally tone-deaf. For instance, laying off workers via email may be efficient, but it lacks humanity. A leader with EI knows that difficult news requires empathy, presence, and respect.

Daniel Goleman, who popularized the concept, said, *"If your emotional abilities aren't in hand…no matter how smart you are, you are not going to get very far."*

Consider *Satya Nadella* at **Microsoft**. Early in his tenure, he emphasized empathy as a leadership value. This wasn't softness—it was strategy. Under his leadership, Microsoft shifted toward a culture of listening, inclusion, and trust, which helped fuel one of the most successful turnarounds in modern business history.

EI also helps leaders balance justice with compassion. Suppose an employee breaks a rule.

EI helps a leader ask: *Why? What pressures led to this choice? How can accountability be paired with growth?*

The answer may be discipline, but delivered with understanding, rather than humiliation.

As Maya Angelou reminded us, *"People will forget what you said, people will forget what you did, but people will never forget how you made them feel."*

Practical step: Before making your next tough decision, pause and ask yourself: *Am I choosing only with my head, or also with my heart?*

Activities for Reflection and Action

Putting ethics into practice requires consistent habits, not just lofty ideas. These activities allow you to test real situations, reflect on choices, and build moral strength through daily actions.

1. **Gray Zone Test**

- **Activity:** Pick one recent decision where the "right" answer wasn't obvious (conflict of priorities, pressure, or limited data). Run it through this chapter's four-step lens: (1) Clarify the stakeholders, (2) Check the stated values + policy, (3) Seek transparency (what would you be comfortable sharing), (4) Choose the long-term good.

- **Action:** Write a 3–5 sentence "decision memo" you could read aloud to your team explaining the choice and the why. File it in a shared folder for future reference.

- **Reflection:** Did the extra transparency or long-term focus change your call? If yes, note what you'll do differently next time when a gray zone appears.

2. The Integrity Mirror

- **Activity:** List the top three leadership calls your team has seen from you in the last 90 days (budget, hiring, vendor, timelines). For each, circle one: *Proud to explain publicly / Would feel defensive*.

- **Action:** Pick one you circled "defensive." Decide a corrective step you can take this week (clarify context to the team, reverse or revise, or add a safeguard so it doesn't repeat). Put a due date on it.

- **Reflection:** After the corrective step, ask two team members privately: "Did this action rebuild confidence?" Capture their verbatim input.

3. Code-to-Conduct Gap Scan

- **Activity:** Choose three lines from your Code of Conduct (e.g., conflicts of interest, fair opportunity, data privacy). Observe one typical week of *"real life"*: meetings, emails, Slack, dashboards. Where do daily behaviors drift from the code?

- **Action:** Close one gap with a small system tweak (e.g., add a conflict-of-interest checkbox to vendor forms; require a second reviewer for sensitive data pulls; introduce structured turns so quieter voices speak in meetings). Announce the tweak and why you made it.

- **Reflection:** What behavior was your system *really* rewarding—speed, secrecy, or silence? What metric or incentive can you re-align to reward the ethical behavior you want?

4. **Emotional Compass Pause**

   - **Activity:** Before your next tough call, prepare a two-column note: **Head** (facts, risks, laws, numbers) and **Heart** (people affected, emotions, dignity, timing). Add a third line: **Humanity test** — "If I were on the receiving end, would I feel respected?"

     - **Action:** Adjust your plan by 10% to honor the human impact (timing, tone, support, or mitigation). Example: announce a change on a Wednesday with live Q&A and a follow-up resource pack, instead of a Friday email.

     - **Reflection:** Did the small humane adjustment increase trust or cooperation? Capture one observable sign (questions asked, tone in replies, speed of alignment).

5. **Speak-Up Pulse (Psychological Safety Check)**

- **Activity:** Send a 5-question, 1–5 scale pulse (anonymous):

  - I feel safe raising concerns here.

  - Leaders explain the "why" behind tough decisions.

  - Ethics matter as much as results do.

  - We correct mistakes, without blame.

  - I know how to escalate concerns, if needed.

- **Action:** Share the results—warts and all—in your next meeting. Choose one improvement you'll put on trial for 30 days (e.g., a rotating "red flag" agenda slot).

- **Reflection:** What surprised you most? Note down one sentence that you will use consistently, to normalize candor (e.g., "Thank you for naming that—let's work the problem—not the person!").

6. **Moral Courage Reps (Escalation Practice)**

- **Activity:** With a trusted peer, role-play two scenarios: (a) a beloved top performer violates a policy, (b) a senior stakeholder pressures you to *"bend"* a control.

Practice saying *no* with respect and offering a principled alternative.

- **Action:** Script two 30-second *"courage lines"* you can use verbatim when pressure hits (e.g., "I can't approve this as-is because it breaks our commitment to X. Here's a compliant path that still gets us Y.").

- **Reflection:** After your next real-world test, jot what worked, what felt hard, and which ally you'll loop in earlier next time.

7. **Ethical Risk Radar (Proactive Scan)**

- **Activity:** Map the top five ethical risks for your team this quarter (data use, vendor selection, incentives, confidentiality, conflicts). For each, note triggers, early warnings, and current controls.

- **Action:** Add one *preventive* control (pre-read checklist, dual-approval, red-team review, or a "cool-off" period before finalizing high-pressure deals).

- **Reflection:** Which single control most reduced your stress? Keep it and sunset a low-value rule to avoid process bloat.

Your Path Forward: Living Ethics Every Day

Ethics is not a checkbox. It is a daily discipline, a backbone strengthened with every decision. The resilient leader does not wait for big crises to demonstrate integrity—they build it in small moments: honoring promises, listening openly, treating others with respect.

Think of ethics as a **muscle.** Every time you choose the harder right over the easier wrong, the muscle strengthens. It grows steadier every time you pause to reflect instead of rushing. Every time you encourage honesty, instead of punishing it, your **backbone** becomes harder to break.

As <u>Simon Sinek</u> put it, *"Integrity is when our words and deeds are consistent with our intentions."*

Carry these truths with you:

- ***Frameworks** turn foggy gray zones into green lights.*

- ***Integrity** builds trust that outlasts profit cycles.*

- ***Ethical culture** lives in the daily, not just in the written.*

- ***Emotional intelligence** gives morality its human compass.*

So, the real question for you is this: When people look back on your leadership, will they say you delivered results—or will they say you delivered results with integrity?

That is the path to building not only successful leaders, but also enduring legacies...

Chapter 5
Leadership Under Fire: Ethical Decision-Making in Crucible Moments

Introduction

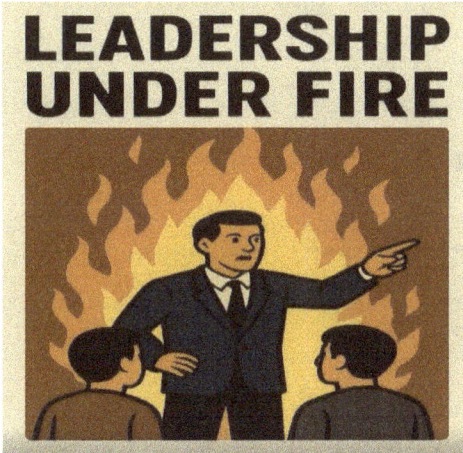

Leadership is not defined by calm seasons of routine—it is tested in fire! The moments of greatest stress, when choices carry heavy consequences, reveal who a leader truly is. These crucible moments are not about efficiency or profit margins; they are about character, courage, and the strength to stand by values when everything else seems to shake.

<u>James Lane Allen</u> once said, *"Adversity does not build character, it reveals it."*

This truth is at the heart of leadership under fire. A leader's character may be polished in good times, but it is exposed during trials. How leaders respond in those critical moments—whether they compromise their values for convenience or hold fast to their principles—determines not only their legacy, but also the destiny of those they lead.

This chapter explores the art of making ethical decisions under pressure. We will explore practical ways to resolve dilemmas, learn how to resist short-term temptations, examine the consequences of ignoring ethics, and understand how to neutralize toxic influences. These are not distant theories—they are essential persistence skills for modern leadership.

Pause for reflection: *When you think of the greatest leaders you admire, do you remember their strategies— or their courage under fire?*

Navigating the Maze: A Practical Leadership Guide to Resolving Ethical Dilemmas

Ethical dilemmas rarely arrive neatly labeled as right versus wrong. They are more often right versus right, or right versus almost right. They live in the messy in-between, where leaders must weigh competing values and uncertain outcomes.

The Greek philosopher Heraclitus once observed, *"Character is destiny."*

In ethical dilemmas, this truth becomes visible. A leader's choices in gray zones do not just resolve problems; they shape reputation and influence the long-term path of the organization.

To navigate these dilemmas, leaders can follow a simple but disciplined process:

1. ***Clarify the Conflict:*** *Name the values in tension. For example, are you torn between transparency and confidentiality, or fairness and speed?*

2. ***Seek Counsel:*** *Bring in trusted voices who can challenge assumptions and broaden perspective. Ethical leadership is rarely built in isolation.*

3. ***Examine Consequences:*** *Look beyond the immediate. What unintended ripple effects could this decision cause? Will it still feel right in five years?*

4. ***Apply the "Sunlight Test":*** *Imagine your decision was printed on the front page of tomorrow's newspaper. Would you still make it?*

5. ***Act with Ownership:*** *Once a decision is made, communicate it openly, and accept full responsibility for both outcome and process.*

Consider the example of a company that is considering whether to recall a product that has shown rare but harmful defects. Legally, they may not be obligated, but ethically, they must ask: *"If this were my child using this product, what would I expect the company to do?"* That single perspective can illuminate the maze more than endless cost-benefit spreadsheets.

Ethical dilemmas will never offer perfect answers. But leaders who approach them with discipline, humility, and courage ensure that even imperfect choices are made with integrity.

The Pressure Test: Resisting Short-Term Gains for Long-Term Leadership Integrity

Pressure does strange things to people. It accelerates decisions, narrows focus, and tempts leaders to take shortcuts that they would never consider in calmer times. Yet it is precisely under pressure that integrity matters most.

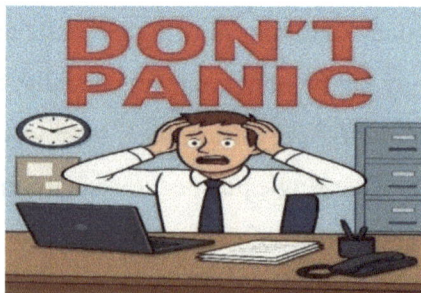

"No panic," he said — moments before the network had other plans.

During a major system outage, a department head proudly declared, "No panic — we'll handle this with calm leadership and clear communication." Ten minutes later, his calm voice echoed across the building as he shouted, "Does anyone know how to reboot a server before the entire client database evaporates?"

The irony wasn't lost on his team. What began as a stressful situation turned into a valuable demonstration: integrity under fire isn't about pretending to be unshakable — it's about staying transparent, composed, and honest when things unravel. The team's laughter, once the crisis passed, became a reminder that real leadership doesn't eliminate chaos; it steadies people through it.

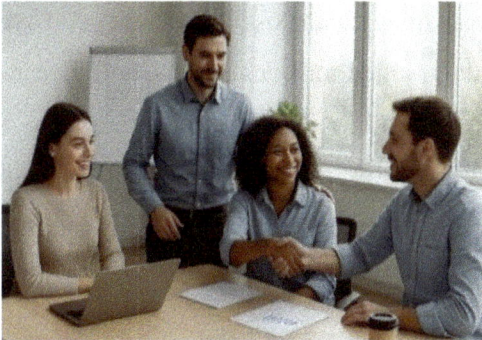

Crisis resolved — leadership recovered, and calm was finally restored (for real this time)

Thomas Paine once wrote, "These are the times that try men's souls."

Leadership is tried not in moments of comfort, but in the crucible of urgency. When deadlines loom, investors demand returns, or competitors seem to be gaining ground, the easiest path is to compromise. But every shortcut has a hidden cost, and that cost is trust.

History proves this again and again. The *2008 financial collapse* was fueled by organizations prioritizing immediate gains through reckless lending, rather than safeguarding long-term stability. The collapse did not stem from lack of knowledge—it stemmed from failure of courage!

Also consider **Toyota's** *Recall Crisis* in 2010, involving defective accelerator pedals, which led to unintended acceleration, and improperly placed floor mats. This had safety implications. Initially, Toyota was reluctant to accept responsibility and downplayed the issue, but upon government investigations, fines, and loss of business, Toyota publicly admitted fault, recalled millions of cars, and invested heavily in quality control reforms. The short-term damage to sales and reputation was sharp, but their (eventual) transparency and accountability restored customer trust, allowing them to remain one of the top automakers globally.

When under pressure, leaders must ask themselves:

- *Does this decision protect or endanger the long-term reputation of our organization?*

- *Am I choosing convenience over conviction?*

- *Would my future self-thank me—or regret me—for what I decide today?*

Integrity may not yield the fastest gains, but it yields the most enduring ones. A leader's willingness to pass the pressure test shows followers that values are not seasonal slogans—they are unshakable commitments.

> **Reflect on this:** *What is one area in your current leadership role where pressure tempts you to take shortcuts? How would it look to resist and instead invest in long-term integrity?*

Case Studies in Crisis: Leadership Lessons from the Fall of Giants

The collapse of powerful institutions often shocks the world, but in hindsight, the causes are rarely surprising. Beneath their glossy surfaces, ethical cracks were already spreading.

Albert Einstein once said, *"Whoever is careless with the truth in small matters cannot be trusted with important matters."*

This insight explains why once-great companies like Lehman Brothers, Boeing, and Theranos fell so dramatically—their leaders tolerated small compromises until those compromises consumed the culture.

- ***Lehman Brothers (2008):*** *Once a pillar of Wall Street, Lehman fueled the housing bubble with reckless risk-*

taking and opaque financial products. When the market shifted, their fragile empire imploded, triggering a global crisis.

Lesson: Short-term gains built on hidden risks create long-term devastation.

- **Boeing (737 MAX Crisis, 2018–2019):** *Pressured to compete with Airbus, Boeing rushed its 737 MAX to market. Flawed software and inadequate pilot training contributed to two deadly crashes. Lives were lost, and trust in the brand plummeted.*

  Lesson: When speed and profit outweigh safety, both people and reputations pay the price.

- **Theranos (2015–2018):** *Hailed as a healthcare revolutionary, Theranos promised life-saving blood tests with just a finger prick. Behind the scenes, the technology never worked. Years of secrecy and deception unraveled into criminal charges.*

  Lesson: Charisma cannot cover for truth—eventually, reality breaks through the illusion.

These collapses remind leaders that culture is not built by slogans on walls, but by daily decisions at every level. If those decisions tolerate corner-cutting, eventually the whole structure gives way.

The fall of giants is less a mystery than a mirror. Leaders who study them are not asked to feel pity, but to feel urgency: *"Are there small compromises in my world today that could become scandals tomorrow?"*

Neutralizing Toxic Influence: A Guide to Anti-Bullying Leadership

Not all crises come from external scandals. Many begin quietly inside organizations, fueled by toxic individuals who bully, manipulate, or create fear. Their influence corrodes morale and stifles innovation.

Hannah Arendt once observed, *"The sad truth is that most evil is done by people who never make up their minds to be good or evil."*

In workplaces, toxicity often thrives, not because people choose it openly, but because leaders fail to confront it.

Neutralizing toxic influence requires leaders to act with clarity and courage:

1. ***Set the Standard:*** *Make it clear that no level of performance excuses bullying or intimidation.*

2. ***Model the Culture:*** *Demonstrate respect in every interaction, especially under stress. Culture follows example more than policy.*

67

3. ***Protect Whistleblowers:*** *Ensure employees have safe ways to raise concerns, without fear of retaliation.*

4. ***Empower the Silent:*** *Look for those who rarely speak in meetings—silence often signals fear. Invite their voices to be heard.*

Consider the story of a tech company, where a top performer routinely humiliated colleagues in meetings. Leadership excused the behavior because *"he delivered results."*

Within three years, employee turnover spiked, innovation slowed, and the company lost its reputation as a great place to work. By tolerating one toxic star, leaders dimmed the light of an entire culture.

Ethical leadership recognizes that toxicity is not just an interpersonal issue—it is a strategic risk!

Culture is either guarded or it decays. Leaders must remember: silence is not neutrality; silence is complicity.

Look closely: *Are there behaviors in your environment today that people "explain away" because of performance? What would courage look like in addressing them?*

Activities for Reflection & Action:

Crucible moments demand more than theory—they require practice. These simple activities will help you pause, reflect, and put ethical leadership into action, so that when the pressure comes, your choices are guided by clarity, courage, and conviction.

1. **The Sunlight Test**

   - Activity: Think of a current decision you're facing. Imagine it on tomorrow's front page.

   - Action: If you would hesitate to defend it publicly, pause and adjust your choice.

2. **The Pressure Audit**

   - Activity: Identify one area where you feel pressed to chase quick results.

   - Action: Write one concrete step you can take to protect long-term trust instead.

3. **Crisis Case Reflection**

   - Activity: Pick one case study from this chapter (Boeing, Uber, BP). Ask: What mistake would I be most likely to repeat under pressure?

   - Action: Create a safeguard now to prevent it.

4. **Toxicity Check**

- Activity: List any behaviors in your team that quietly erode morale—fear, favoritism, or silence.

- Action: Choose one behavior and address it directly this week.

5. **Legacy Lens**

- Activity: Write down three words you want people to use about your leadership in a crisis.

- Action: Ask yourself each day: Did my actions move me closer to that legacy?

The Rock or the Sand?

Crucible moments are unavoidable. They are the storm clouds of leadership, revealing who is anchored by values and who drifts with convenience. Some leaders will emerge scarred but stronger; others will be undone by compromises too small to notice until it's too late.

Viktor Frankl, who survived the crucible of the Holocaust, wrote, *"When we are no longer able to change a situation, we are challenged to change ourselves."*

Leaders may not control the crises that confront them, but they can control the integrity with which they respond.

The path ahead requires courage. Leaders must:

- *Navigate dilemmas with frameworks that prioritize clarity over confusion.*

- *Resist the lure of short-term comfort in favor of long-term trust.*

- *Learn from the collapse of giants and guard against small cracks in their own walls.*

- *Neutralize toxic influence before it spreads, remembering that culture is built in daily choices.*

The crucible is an opportunity, rather than a curse. It allows leaders to prove to themselves and to others that their values are more than just words—that they are lived commitments, even when they are costly.

Final challenge: *When your next test of fire arrives, will you be remembered as a leader who succumbed under pressure, or one who stood like a rock of integrity in the storm?*

Part 3

The Adaptive Leadership Arena

Chapter 6
The Adaptive Enterprise: Leadership for Today's Business Models

Introduction

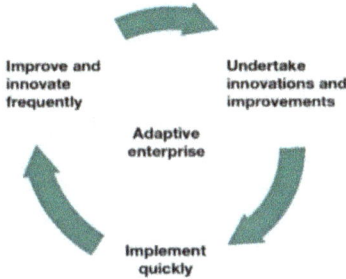

The modern business world does not sit still. The landscape shifts constantly—new technologies, evolving customer expectations, changing family dynamics, and global disruptions. Leaders today must carry a skillset beyond vision and authority—they must carry adaptability! The ability to bend without breaking, to pivot without losing purpose, and to stay grounded when the ground beneath them is shifting is what sets apart the leaders who thrive from those who falter.

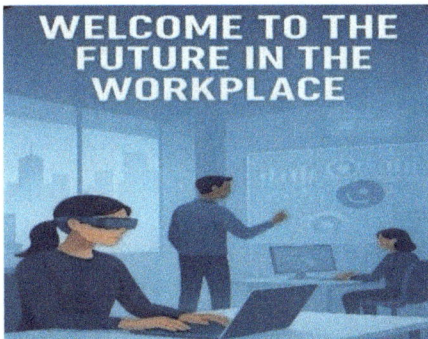

"Welcome to the future"—and goodbye to every chair in the building.

When one company announced its grand "Adaptability Drive," the CEO decided to prove the point by replacing the entire office with a fully remote setup overnight. Desks vanished, printers disappeared, and a note on the door cheerfully read, *"Welcome to the future—work from anywhere!"*

The only problem? Half the staff arrived that morning without laptops, and the company Wi-Fi hadn't yet been configured for remote access. Within hours, calls came from parking lots, cafés, and one particularly resourceful accountant who turned her car trunk into a mobile desk.

By noon, the CEO called everyone back to the office, reinstated the desks, and simply said, "Lesson learned: adaptability works better when the Wi-Fi does." The team laughed—but they also saw the truth. Change succeeds not because it's fast, but because it's thought through with people in mind.

Charles Darwin once reminded us, *"It is not the strongest of the species that survives, nor the most intelligent, but the one most responsive to change."*

It's the same with leadership – adaptability is what keeps you going.

This chapter looks at four distinct but interconnected arenas of leadership today:

- *The **independent professional** is climbing the mountain solo.*

- *The **legacy family enterprise**, where history and emotion run deep.*

- *The **critical handoff of succession**, when the torch must be passed.*

- *The **role of communication** (delicate yet powerful) in family business.*

Together, they reveal how leadership must adapt, evolve, and reimagine itself while still holding fast to its ethical foundations.

Pause for reflection: *When change knocks on your door, do you open with curiosity—or brace yourself with resistance?*

The Solo Ascent: Mastering Leadership as an Independent Professional

Leading alone can feel like climbing a mountain with no trail markers. Independent professionals—consultants, freelancers, small business owners—are their own strategist, executor, marketer, and financial officer. Success or failure falls entirely on their shoulders.

This kind of leadership requires stamina and discipline. There is no board of directors to provide feedback, no HR department to handle conflict, no mentor waiting in the next office. The independent leader must build his or her own support system.

Henry David Thoreau once said, *"The price of anything is the amount of life you exchange for it."*

For solo leaders, every hour spent must be weighed carefully. The temptation to chase every opportunity is strong, but the wiser path is focus—saying "no" often enough to ensure that the *"yes"* carries weight.

Independent leadership brings unique challenges:

- ***Isolation:*** *Without colleagues to brainstorm with, decision-making can feel lonely. Independent leaders must intentionally create networks of peers or mentors.*

- ***Burnout Risk:*** *Without clear boundaries, work efficiency expands to fill every waking moment. Solo leaders need rest as much as productivity.*

- ***Resource Limits:*** *With limited budgets and small teams, independent leaders must be creative while optimizing resources without compromising quality.*

Yet the rewards are truly immense! Climbing solo gives you incredible freedom and a real sense of personal achievement. You get to decide not only how you work, but also how to shape your business to reflect what matters most to you.

Take the story of an ***independent graphic designer*** who turned down a lucrative contract with a tobacco company, despite the financial pressure she faced. She explained later, *"I wanted to build a career I could tell my kids about with pride."*

That choice, costly in the moment, led to clients who admired her integrity and brought her work that better matched her values.

> **Consider this:** *If you are climbing the solo mountain, what kind of "yes" do you want your work to represent—and what "no" do you need the courage to say?*

The Legacy Business: The Unique Challenge of Family Enterprise Leadership

Family businesses are unlike any other. They carry not only financial assets, but also emotional legacies. They hold within them the hopes of previous generations, the pride of a family name, and the pressure to preserve what has been built.

As Warren Buffett once said, *"Someone is sitting in the shade today because someone planted a tree a long time ago."*

Family enterprise leaders sit in that shade. But they also carry the responsibility of planting new trees for those who will come after them.

The challenge lies in balancing two powerful forces: tradition and change. Family businesses often have deep roots in values, culture, and identity. However, in a fast-changing market, those same roots can sometimes hinder leaders from embracing necessary innovation.

Consider a **third-generation family bakery in Chicago**. The grandfather built it on authenticity and hand-crafted recipes. The granddaughter, now at the helm, saw the need to expand online and adapt to new health-conscious customers. Tension rose at family dinners when she suggested offering gluten-free bread. *"That's not real bread!"* her uncle protested. But eventually, the compromise of offering both traditional and modern options allowed the bakery to thrive without betraying its roots.

Family businesses also face the challenge of blurred boundaries. Conversations about sales figures and succession often spill over into holiday gatherings. Emotional baggage from personal life can cloud professional judgment. Leaders must learn to separate *"family table" from "boardroom table."*

Another challenge is the temptation of favoritism. Appointing relatives to leadership roles based solely on family ties, undermines the business's credibility. The strongest family enterprises adopt professional governance—clear role definitions, external advisors, and fair performance measures.

Passing the Torch: A Contemporary Guide to Succession Leadership

No leader leads forever. Eventually, the torch must be passed. Yet succession remains one of the most neglected responsibilities of leadership. Too often, leaders invest in growth strategies, but fail to invest in preparing the next generation to carry the torch.

Peter Drucker observed, *"There is no success without a successor."*

Leadership is incomplete if it dies with the current leader.

Effective succession is less about finding the right replacement at the last minute and more about preparing a fertile environment where new leaders can flourish. It involves mentoring, deliberate exposure to challenges, and gradual handoff of responsibility.

Consider the contrast between *two mid-sized companies*. In one, the founder held on tightly until his late seventies, refusing to share power. When he passed away, his children were unprepared, infighting broke out, and the business declined sharply. In the other, the founder began a transition plan a decade earlier, slowly introducing the next generation to decision-making, while bringing in outside expertise. When he stepped aside, the transition was seamless.

Succession is also about letting go with grace. Leaders often see their organizations as extensions of themselves. Handing over control feels like losing identity. Yet clinging too long can suffocate the very growth that leaders once nurtured.

A *family-owned vineyard in California* offers a good example. The father had built the business from scratch, pouring decades of his life into the soil. When his daughter expressed interest in leading, he hesitated because he was afraid that she would not meet his standards.

However, over time, he began to let her lead harvest operations, negotiate contracts, and eventually manage the entire enterprise. *"I realized,"* he later reflected, *"that my greatest legacy wasn't the wine I made—it was her capacity to carry the vineyard further than I ever could."*

Difficult Conversations: Mastering Communication for Family Business Leadership

Of all the challenges in family enterprise leadership, communication is often the most difficult. Conversations about money, control, and succession are rarely just about business—they are about identity, fairness, and a sense of belonging.

George Bernard Shaw once quipped, *"The single biggest problem in communication is the illusion that it has taken place."*

In family businesses, silence is often mistaken for agreement, when in reality it breeds resentment. Difficult conversations cannot be avoided. They must be approached with courage and care.

This involves:

- **Radical Transparency:** *Saying clearly what others tiptoe around. Half-truths solve nothing.*

- **Empathy First:** *Listening to feelings before proposing solutions. A brother who feels overlooked will not hear strategy until he feels understood.*

- **Structured Dialogue:** *Using facilitators, advisors, or written agreements to ensure clarity and reduce ambiguity.*

One **retail family chain** illustrates this well. The second generation assumed that leadership would pass by birth order, while the third generation quietly resented being excluded from the decision-making process. Tension simmered for years until an outside advisor was brought in. Through structured conversations, roles and responsibilities were clarified, and succession was mapped transparently. The family later reflected that the business was saved not by strategy, but by honest dialogue.

Communication is not just about words; it is about trust! When family members know that they can speak openly without judgment, the business gains resilience. When conversations are avoided, cracks deepen until they split both family and enterprise apart.

Reflection: *What is one difficult conversation you have avoided because it feels uncomfortable? How might your leadership grow stronger if you faced it directly?*

Activities for Reflection & Action:

Leadership involves practicing ideas, not just understanding them. This section provides activities to test adaptability, improve decision-making, and apply lessons daily—like a toolkit for lasting change.

1. **The Solo Audit**

   - *Activity:* List the top three ways in which you spend your time as an independent leader.

   - *Action:* Circle one way that drains you without aligning to your values. What would it look like to say "no" to it?

2. **Legacy Balance Check**

   - *Activity:* Write down three traditions that your family business values most.

   - *Action:* Evaluate: are they anchoring stability, or blocking innovation? Decide which to preserve, and which to adapt.

3. **Succession Scorecard**

   - *Activity:* On a scale of 1–10, how ready is your organization for leadership transition?

- *Action:* If under 7, identify one future leader and commit to mentoring him or her in a new responsibility this month.

4. **Courageous Conversation Plan**

   - *Activity:* Identify one family or business conversation that you have avoided.

   - *Action:* Note down three bullet points: what needs to be said, how you will say it, and the outcome you hope for. Schedule the talk.

5. **Adaptability Lens**

   - *Activity:* Ask yourself, 'Where am I resisting change?'

   - *Action:* Write one small adjustment you can make this week, to lean into flexibility without losing your values.

Adapting Without Losing Ground

Adaptability is no longer optional—it is a matter of survival! Whether you are leading as an independent professional, guiding a family enterprise, preparing for succession, or engaging in complex conversations, the ability to shift with humility, while holding true to your values, defines enduring leadership.

As basketball coach <u>John Wooden</u> once said, *"Flexibility is the key to stability."*

The adaptive enterprise is not about chasing every trend or abandoning tradition. It is about knowing when to bend and when to stand firm. It is about planting new trees while honoring the old ones. It is about shaping a future where values are not sacrificed, but strengthened.

Final Challenge: *Look honestly at your leadership today. Where do you need more flexibility? And what one step can you take this week to adapt without losing your foundation?*

Leaders who adapt without losing core values build enterprises that thrive amid change...

Chapter 7
The Sustainable Self: Leadership Strategies for Well-being and Success

Introduction

In today's fast-moving business climate, leadership is not just about delivering results—*it's about sustaining the self that provides them.* Leaders find themselves juggling several balls because they are faced with endless demands: meeting quarterly targets, addressing social concerns, navigating digital change, and managing crises.

However, in the rush to serve others, many leaders overlook the most vital responsibility of all: *Caring for themselves.*

Here's the truth: *A leader who is drained cannot pour into others.*

"Time to Rest, Team!" — sent just before sunrise.

One company launched a "Wellness Week" to promote rest and work-life balance. Posters went up, emails went out, and the CEO sent an all-staff message at 2:47 a.m. announcing the campaign with the subject line: *"Time to Rest, Team!"*

By morning, employees replied with gentle humor — a few even attached screenshots of the timestamp. The irony wasn't lost on anyone, least of all the CEO, who later admitted with a grin, "Maybe I should start by closing my own laptop before midnight."

The moment became a small but meaningful turning point. The following month, late-night emails stopped, meeting hours shortened, and the message shifted from slogans to practice. Everyone learned that sustainability begins not with policy, but with example.

Exhaustion clouds judgment, weakens empathy, and narrows vision. The organizations that they lead begin to mirror that depletion. By contrast, leaders who cultivate sustainable practices—*mentally, emotionally, and physically*—become steady anchors for their teams.

Anne Lamott captured it beautifully when she said, *"Almost everything will work again if you unplug it for a few minutes, including you."*

Sustainable leadership means learning how to unplug, recharge, and lead from a place of fullness rather than depletion.

This chapter focuses on four crucial practices: building resilience beyond burnout, decoding anger as a constructive signal, protecting teams from the myth of the *"always-right"* customer, and designing a life where fulfillment and leadership co-exist.

Pause for reflection: *When was the last time you treated your well-being as seriously as you treat a board meeting?*

Beyond Burnout: Resilience Strategies for Individual and Organizational Leadership

Burnout is not simply a heavy workload. It is a chronic depletion of the spirit—*when leaders find themselves detached, exhausted, and questioning whether their work matters.* Burnout shows up as constant fatigue, irritability, loss of focus, or even a quiet numbness that makes success feel hollow.

Burnout doesn't only hurt the leader. It sends shockwaves across teams. Employees often mirror their leader's state. When the leader runs on fumes, the culture absorbs the message that exhaustion is the expected standard.

As Arianna Huffington put it, *"We think, mistakenly, that success is the result of the amount of time we put in at work, instead of the quality of time we put in."*

True resilience requires a shift in mindset: rest is not wasted time, but a renewable source of clarity and creativity.

Personal Strategies for Resilience

1. ***Rest as Non-Negotiable:*** *Leaders must reframe sleep, breaks, and downtime as strategic assets. Great athletes rest to perform; great leaders must too.*

2. ***Boundaries as Armor:*** *Leadership today comes with a 24/7 digital tether. Without firm boundaries—no-phone dinners, email cutoffs, quiet weekends—the line between work and life evaporates.*

3. ***Recovery Rituals:*** *Rituals like daily walks, journaling, meditation, or creative hobbies restore balance. These habits are not indulgences but reinforcements.*

Organizational Strategies for Resilience

1. ***Cultural Modeling:*** *Employees mimic leaders. If leaders send midnight emails, staff learn exhaustion is the standard. Modeling balance is an act of cultural leadership.*

2. ***Flexible Work Structures:*** *Remote work, wellness programs, and respect for time off ensure resilience is systemic —not optional!*

3. ***Shared Ownership:*** *When leaders delegate effectively, they prevent burnout in themselves and create growth opportunities for others.*

Consider a *healthcare CEO* who noticed her staff was showing signs of deep exhaustion during the pandemic. Instead of pushing harder, she introduced *"recovery Fridays"* once a month, where meetings were banned and staff could use the time for wellness, family, or creative work. Engagement scores increased, and so did productivity. She later reflected, *"I had to learn that protecting people's rest was protecting the mission itself."*

Consider this: *What is one boundary you can set this week that will protect your energy and model resilience for your team?*

The Anger Signal: How Effective Leadership Decodes Emotions for Constructive Action

Leaders often carry the myth that they must be endlessly calm. But anger, when decoded, can be a vital signal. It points toward violated values, unspoken boundaries, or systemic injustices. Left unmanaged, anger corrodes relationships; channeled wisely, it drives transformation.

Maya Angelou once observed, *"Bitterness is like cancer. It eats upon the host. But anger is like fire. It burns it all clean."*

In leadership, controlled anger can be the fire that clears complacency and sparks reform.

Constructive Use of Anger:

1. **Pause Before Reacting:** *Rash reactions often damage trust. Leaders who pause turn heat into clarity.*

2. **Identify the Core Value:** *Anger often masks the deeper principle being violated—respect, fairness, safety. Naming it allows leaders to address the real issue.*

3. **Translate to Action:** *Once clarified, anger should fuel strategy. Redirect the energy into structural fixes, not personal attacks.*

For example, a **school** *superintendent* found out that minority students in her district were being disciplined more often than others. She initially felt very upset about this unfair situation. Instead of blaming, she took a moment to reflect, identified the core value that was affected—*equity*—and took positive steps to make things better. She introduced bias training, updated policies, and provided more support for teachers. Her passion for justice turned her anger into a powerful force for positive change.

Leadership that pretends emotions do not exist creates sterile, disconnected organizations. Leadership that acknowledges emotions—and channels them constructively—creates authentic cultures where values are lived.

> **Think about it:** *When was the last time anger pointed you toward a truth you needed to confront? Did you use it to ignite change or to scorch relationships?*

The Myth of the "Always-Right" Customer: A Leadership Approach to Protecting Your Team

The phrase *"the customer is always right"* has been repeated for decades, but leaders today know it is a dangerous half-truth. Blindly elevating customers above employees, or other stakeholders, creates toxic service environments, fuels burnout, and undermines dignity.

Instead, sustainable leadership recognizes that customer satisfaction and the well-being of other stakeholders must be held in balance. If leaders sacrifice one for the other, the business organization will eventually collapse.

Barbara Corcoran, real estate entrepreneur, once remarked, *"Don't you dare underestimate the power of your own instinct."*

For leaders, instinct often tells them when a customer has crossed the line. Listening to that instinct can save a culture.

Protecting Employees While Serving Customers:

1. ***Set Clear Boundaries:*** *No amount of revenue justifies tolerating abuse or harassment from customers.*

2. ***Back Your People:*** *Employees (and other stakeholders) must know that leaders will defend their dignity publicly when the behavior of customers is out of line.*

3. ***Redefine Success:*** *Metrics should measure not only customer satisfaction, but also the satisfaction of other*

stakeholders. They should reflect employee engagement and workplace respect as well.

For example, at a **midwestern** *restaurant chain*, a regular customer frequently berated the server. Instead of bending over backward to please him, the general manager pulled him aside and said, *"Our team deserves respect. If that doesn't work for you, we'll gladly serve you elsewhere."* The staff later said that moment did more to build loyalty than any bonus.

Leaders who protect their teams send a message: *This is not only a place where customers are valued—it is a place where people are safe.*

When employees feel protected, they serve customers with far greater dedication.

Look closely: *If the members of your team faced a toxic customer tomorrow, would they feel confident that you would defend them?*

Life by Design: Integrating Personal Fulfillment with Professional Leadership

Too often, leaders achieve success on paper but experience emptiness inside. They deliver results, but miss joy. They accumulate achievements, but lose touch with relationships, health, or passions that once mattered most. Sustainable leadership asks: *how can life and leadership be designed as one, integrated whole?*

Steve Jobs once said, *"Your work is going to fill a large part of your life… and the only way to be truly satisfied is to do what you believe is great work."*

But great leadership is not only about loving work—it is about shaping a life that feels whole.

Principles of Life by Design:

1. ***Values First:*** *Start with personal values, then align work decisions accordingly. Without alignment, success feels hollow.*

2. ***Deliberate Joy:*** *Schedule joy with the same seriousness as board meetings—time with family, hobbies, travel, or community.*

3. ***Integration, Not Balance:*** *Instead of chasing perfect balance, look for integration—work that enriches life, and life that energizes work.*

For example, a *financial executive* of a **large enterprise** once admitted that he nearly lost touch with his children during his busiest decade. To reset, he began blocking *"sacred hours"* each week—*soccer games, family dinners, weekends unplugged.* Surprisingly, his leadership sharpened. *"I thought my company would suffer if I worked less,"* he said. *"Instead, I became sharper, calmer, and more creative."*

Life by design is not about having it all—it's about having what matters most, intentionally.

Reflection & Action for Building the Sustainable Self:

This section turns principles into practice. Each exercise is designed to help leaders pause, assess, and make intentional choices that protect energy, channel emotions, and integrate well-being with leadership.

1. **Burnout Barometer**

   - *Activity:* Write down your top three warning signs of burnout.

   - *Action:* Design a "rescue plan" for each—whether it's taking a break, asking for help, or resetting expectations.

2. **Anger Decoder**

   - *Activity:* Recall one moment of leadership anger in the past month.

- *Action:* Identify the value behind it. What constructive step could channel it toward change?

3. **Customer-Employee Balance Check**

   - *Activity:* Review your service policies with your team.

   - *Action:* Add one clear safeguard that ensures employee dignity alongside customer care.

4. **Life Design Audit**

   - *Activity:* Map out how you spent the past month—work, relationships, health, passions.

   - *Action:* Block one "non-negotiable" joy activity this week and treat it as seriously as any business deal.

Leading from Wholeness

Sustainable leadership is truly essential—*it's about thriving*, rather than just surviving. When leaders burn out, mishandle their emotions, sacrifice their teams, or ignore their own well-being, they risk weakening the very missions that they are passionate about. Taking care of ourselves and others is key to lasting success. Leaders who invest in resilience, channel emotions constructively, protect their teams, and live intentionally create legacies that last.

As <u>George Eliot </u>once wrote, *"It is never too late to be what you might have been."*

Sustainability isn't about perfection but about daily choices that keep leaders grounded. The sustainable self is stewardship—not selfishness! It is the foundation from which leaders can serve with clarity, compassion, and strength.

> **Challenge yourself:** *This week, what single habit could you adopt—or release—that would move you closer to sustainable leadership?*

Grounded leaders choose sustainability every day…

Chapter 8
The Financial Blueprint: Leadership for a Lasting Impact

Introduction

Every great leader eventually faces a truth: the impact of leadership is not measured only in today's results, but also in tomorrow's inheritance. Financial decisions—*whether personal, organizational, or societal*—become part of the leader's permanent record. They determine whether stability or struggle prevails, whether values endure or fade with time.

This chapter explores the dimension of leadership that too often remains in the background: **the financial legacy.** It is not about greed or accumulation; it is about stewardship and responsibility. The choices leaders make with resources—*how they earn, allocate, save, invest, and pass them on*—become a blueprint that others must live with.

As Eleanor Roosevelt once said, *"The future belongs to those who believe in the beauty of their dreams."*

Yet dreams without financial planning dissolve quickly. Financial leadership ensures those dreams take form, survive, and flourish.

In this final chapter, we will examine four pillars that shape the financial blueprint of lasting leadership:

1. *Financial fluency for leaders.*

2. *The new retirement.*

3. *Estate planning.*

4. *Investing with impact.*

Pause for reflection: *If your leadership ended today, what financial story would others tell about you? A story of clarity and foresight—or of missed opportunities and confusion?*

Financial Fluency for Leaders: A Conceptual Leadership Guide

Leadership without financial literacy is like navigation without a map. Numbers do not tell the whole story, but without them, the story is incomplete. Financial fluency enables leaders to steward resources effectively, ask more informed questions, and ensure that their actions align with long-term objectives.

This fluency goes beyond reading balance sheets. It means understanding how resources are flowing, what trends reveal, and how risks can be anticipated. Financially fluent leaders are better equipped to balance **mission and margin.**

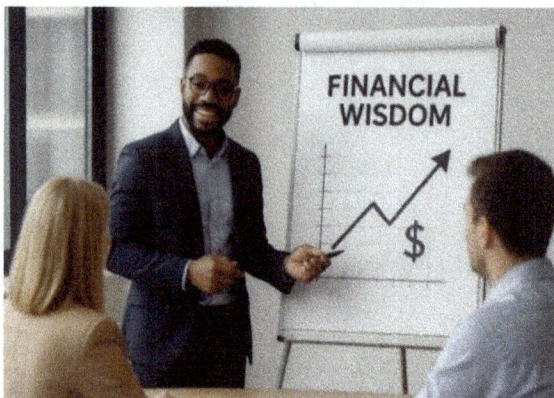

"Every dollar must have a purpose!" — said moments before one literally lost its purpose in a parking meter.

A senior executive once hosted a workshop titled *"Smart Money, Wise Leadership."* He opened with a bold statement: "Every dollar must have a purpose!" and proudly displayed a pie chart showing flawless financial discipline.

Halfway through the session, his assistant quietly entered and whispered, "Sir, your car is being towed — the parking meter expired two hours ago."

The room went silent, then erupted in good-natured laughter. The irony wasn't lost on anyone — a master of macro-finance, outmaneuvered by a micro-budget oversight. The executive chuckled, nodded, and used it as a spontaneous lesson: "Leadership, like finance, is all about paying attention to the small details — or someone else will collect the cost."

That single moment made the message unforgettable. Stewardship isn't about spreadsheets alone; it's about consistency between principle and practice — the everyday habits that protect long-term vision.

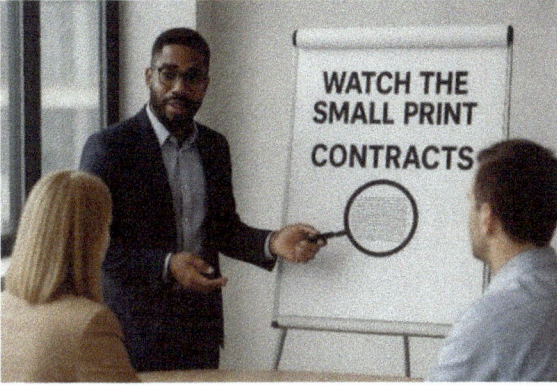

Even the best plans need small-print attention — and a few extra quarters.

Consider Indra Nooyi, former CEO of PepsiCo. Her *"Performance with Purpose"* **strategy** combined financial discipline with sustainability investments. By mastering both the financial and ethical dimensions of leadership, she proved that fluency in numbers empowers leaders to integrate values into business strategy, instead of treating them as optional.

Having **strong financial fluency** allows leaders to spot potential risks early, thereby giving them a valuable edge in decision-making.

For example, the 1997 Asian financial crisis taught many organizations a hard lesson: ignoring currency risks and overleveraging debt can lead to collapse. Financially literate leaders identified the warning signs earlier and planned accordingly.

The New Retirement: A Leadership Approach to Planning for Longevity and Purpose

Retirement used to mean stepping away from productivity into quiet rest. But in today's world—*where leaders live longer and healthier lives*—retirement has evolved into a new season of influence. Financial planning alone is not enough; leaders must also **plan for purpose.**

Longevity brings opportunity; leaders can use retirement years to mentor, write, teach, or invest in causes close to their hearts. Yet without preparation, many experience a loss of identity, drifting without the structure that once gave them meaning.

Nelson Mandela stands as a compelling example. Following his *resignation as South Africa's president*, his post-retirement years were among his most influential, as he continued to advocate for education, peace, and human rights worldwide. His financial stability allowed him to focus on creating a lasting legacy, rather than merely ensuring his own survival.

The new retirement mindset requires **two plans**:

1. *A financial plan that ensures stability and independence.*

2. *A purpose plan that ensures relevance and fulfillment.*

Reflection for you: *If you stepped back tomorrow, would you retire into emptiness—or into an environment where your experience becomes a gift to others?*

Estate Planning as a Final Act of Leadership

Estate planning is more than dividing assets—*it is a final leadership decision about what and who mattered most.* It transforms intentions into lasting structures. When ignored, it leaves behind conflict; when embraced, it leaves behind clarity.

Take the example of <u>Aretha Franklin</u>, who passed away without a **formalized will;** *years of legal disputes among heirs overshadowed her artistic legacy.*

Compare that with <u>Alfred Nobel</u>, who used his **estate to create the Nobel Prizes,** *turning personal wealth into a global engine for progress in science, peace, and literature.* His estate plan truly reflected his lasting leadership and how much he cared about those he left behind.

<u>For leaders, estate planning carries three dimensions:</u>

- *Clarity:* *Reducing confusion through legal documentation.*

- *Continuity:* *Ensuring organizations, families, or charities can carry forward without disruption.*

- **Character:** *Directing resources in ways that reflect values—whether through philanthropy, scholarships, or long-term community investments.*

Reflection for you: *If someone read your will tomorrow, would it echo the values you claimed to stand for in life— or expose gaps between words and priorities?*

Investing with Impact: Aligning Financial Strategy with Ethical Leadership Values

The final piece of the financial blueprint is aligning investments with values. In the past, leaders separated profit-making from purpose-giving. Today, the two are converging. **Impact investing** channels capital into enterprises that generate both financial returns and positive social or environmental impact.

For example, The Rise Fund, which *Bono* and private equity expert *Bill McGlashan* co-founded, invests billions in businesses that enhance education, renewable energy, and healthcare, all while providing competitive returns.

Their model proves that finance can be both **profitable and transformative.**

Impact investing goes beyond **philanthropy**—*it's about being a conscientious steward of resources.*

It invites us to consider: what *if our dollars could promote justice, sustainability, and dignity just as effectively as they generate profit?*

Reflection for you: *If every investment you made were public knowledge, would you be proud of the story your portfolio tells?*

Activities for Reflection and Action:

To help you incorporate these principles into your daily routine, here are some helpful exercises to try out:

1. **Financial Fluency Check**

   - *Activity:* Review the last three financial reports you received. Write down not only the numbers, but the story they tell about health, values, and resilience.

   - *Reflection:* Where do you see alignment with mission—and where do you see drift?

2. **Purposeful Retirement Map**

   - *Activity:* Draft a two-column chart: Column 1 = financial goals, Column 2 = purpose goals.

   - *Action:* Commit to one financial step (e.g., savings increase, debt reduction) and one purpose step (e.g., mentorship, volunteering) this year.

3. **Estate Clarity Scan**

   - *Activity:* List three values you want your estate to reflect.

   - *Action:* Meet with a legal or financial advisor to explore how those values could translate into clear documentation.

4. **Impact Portfolio Audit**

   - *Activity:* Write down your top five current investments.

   - *Action:* Rank them for alignment with your values (High, Medium, Low). Identify one you could replace or adjust for greater alignment.

The Final Ledger: Closing Reflection

Every leader writes two ledgers: *one of* **numbers** *and one of* **legacy**. The financial blueprint captures both. It ensures that prosperity is not squandered, values are not lost, and future generations are not left to rebuild what could have been preserved.

As Jane Goodall once observed, *"You cannot get through a single day without having an impact on the world around you. What you do makes a difference, and you have to decide what kind of difference you want to make."*

<u>Financial leadership is about deciding that difference in tangible ways:</u>

- *By becoming fluent enough to steward resources wisely.*

- *By redefining retirement as purposeful longevity.*

- *By using estate planning to pass on clarity, not conflict.*

- *By investing in a world where capital multiplies both profit and progress.*

This is the closing question for you: *When future generations inherit your blueprint, will they see a map of confusion—or a compass that points to conviction, purpose, and impact?*

Your answer begins today…

Conclusion

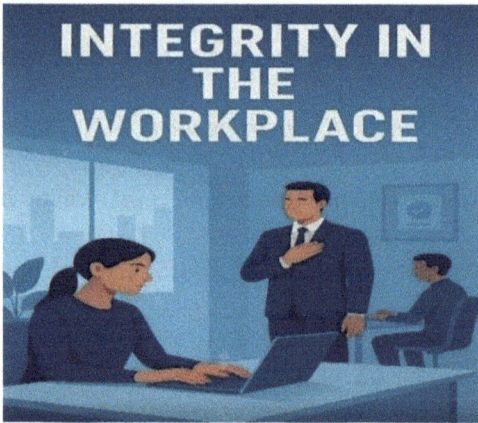

INTEGRITY IN THE WORKPLACE

Leadership in the *twenty-first century* is all about fostering integrity, inspiring vision, and building genuine human connections, especially as our world continues to change so quickly. It's no longer just about asserting authority, boosting profits, or displaying charisma—*it's about leading with authenticity and compassion amidst a constantly evolving global landscape.*

The Ethical Leader's Playbook has explored this transformation through the moral, psychological, and strategic lenses of leadership. As the world continues to shift under the forces of technology, social change, and environmental urgency, today's leaders must rise beyond traditional hierarchies and redefine what success truly means.

At the heart of ethical leadership lies purpose. Chapter 1 began by reminding us that purpose is not a slogan—it is a compass.

Leaders must ensure that the ladder of success they climb rests against the right wall. The "Triple Bottom Line" philosophy—*People, Planet, Purpose*—reframes profit not as the ultimate measure, but as the byproduct of doing what is right.

When leaders recognize that sustainable success relies on caring for employees, communities, and the environment, they become true stewards. Purposeful leadership is practical, not just idealistic. Organizations that align their vision with core values tend to outperform those focused solely on short-term gains. Ultimately, a leader's legacy is defined not by quarterly profits but by the culture and trust they nurture.

Starting from the concept of purpose, we shifted focus to trust—*the human element vital to every organization.* Chapter 2 highlighted that leadership isn't rooted in titles or roles, but in relationships. Trust acts as the unseen link connecting individuals to their work and to each other, flourishing in environments of transparency, empathy, and fairness.

In this chapter, we understand that psychological safety, diversity, and inclusion are fundamental drivers of innovation, not just corporate trends. A trusting environment encourages individuals to voice their ideas, take risks, and be true to themselves at work. Without this trust, creativity diminishes, replaced by fear. Leaders should recognize that their team members are partners in achieving shared goals, not mere productivity tools.

Building on our connection as a foundation, Chapter 3 took a warm look at the art of communication. It emphasized that truly great leaders aren't necessarily the loudest in the room, but those who listen best. In a time when emails often substitute for face-to-face chats and emojis express feelings, having the skill to communicate with genuine empathy truly becomes a superpower.

The concept of *'Digital Body Language'* reminds us that tone, timing, and context are just as important online as they are in person. Leadership communication thrives when honesty is balanced with compassion, when negotiation seeks mutual value, and when trust becomes currency. Words can heal or harm; leaders must wield them as instruments of clarity and care.

Every leadership journey is rooted in a strong ethical foundation. In Chapter 4, we explored how true leadership involves the courage to stand up for what is right, even when others turn away. Ethical leadership begins with a commitment to integrity and ends with taking responsibility. In today's complex business environment—*covering areas like privacy, data management, and environmental decisions*—we need more than just ticking boxes; we need thoughtful engagement.

They require conscience. Integrity is not a soft virtue but a strategic advantage: it builds credibility that no marketing campaign can buy. The emotionally intelligent leader uses both head and heart, pairing logic with empathy to ensure that decisions serve humanity as well as business goals.

When ethics are tested, leadership under fire is uncovered. Chapter 5 reminded us that character is not built in comfort but in crisis. The stories of corporate failures like Enron, Theranos, and Boeing serve as warnings of what happens when moral courage yields to convenience. True leaders avoid the temptation of short-term gains and instead focus on building lasting trust.

They safeguard their teams, prioritize safety, and make transparent decisions, even when it is costly. They eliminate toxic influences, understanding that one unchecked bully can corrupt an entire culture. In critical moments of leadership—*when pressure peaks and visibility is most significant*—values should guide decisions, not emotions or ego.

Having faced the moral fire, Part Three led us into the adaptive arena, where leaders learn to bend without breaking. Chapter 6 examined adaptability as a crucial trait for modern business survival. Whether leading a solo enterprise, managing a family legacy, or orchestrating succession, today's leader must balance flexibility with fidelity to values. Family businesses, for example, remind us that leadership is not just professional — *it is personal*.

Heritage, identity, and emotion intertwine, requiring leaders to communicate thoughtfully and pass the torch wisely. Succession, when approached intentionally, becomes an act of generosity—*a continuation of purpose across generations.*

Chapter 7 moved the lens inward, focusing on the sustainable self—the leader as a human being. Leadership without self-care collapses under its own weight. The myth of the *'always-on'* executive must end. A burnt-out leader cannot inspire resilience in others. Sustainable leadership demands balance: rest as strategy, boundaries as protection, and reflection as renewal. Emotional intelligence once again takes center stage, helping leaders decode anger as a signal for change rather than a symptom of stress.

Likewise, leaders must challenge the outdated belief that *'the customer is always right.'* Protecting the dignity and well-being of employees is as vital as satisfying clients. The chapter closes with *'Life by Design,'* encouraging leaders to integrate fulfillment, faith, and purpose into the fabric of their careers.

The final section, *'The Financial Legacy of Leadership,'* examines how leaders can sustain ethical influence beyond their own lifetimes. Chapter 8 presents financial literacy as a moral duty. Faithful stewardship involves not only earning wisely but also giving meaningfully. Financial fluency enables leaders to make decisions that align with their values, from impact investing to equitable pay.

Reimagined retirement shifts from withdrawal to legacy—*a move from accumulation to contribution.* Estate planning and ethical investing complete the cycle, showing that money, when guided by principles, can extend a leader's impact across generations.

Taken together, the lessons of this playbook reveal that ethical leadership is both an inner discipline and an outer practice. It is as much about *who you are* as *what you do.* It calls for moral courage, self-awareness, and the humility to keep learning. It demands a balance between decisiveness and compassion, vision and adaptability, principle and pragmatism.

An ethical leader isn't a perfect saint, but a dedicated learner—*constantly improving, thinking deeply, and adjusting along the way.* They understand that each email, decision, and meeting is an excellent opportunity to lead with honesty and integrity. Truly ethical leadership starts the moment someone chooses to stay aware rather than be indifferent, to prioritize fairness over fear, and to serve others rather than themselves.

In our rapidly changing world—*faced with technological breakthroughs, environmental challenges, and social divides*—the need for ethical leaders has never been more important. The future isn't just about gathering power, but about wielding it with purpose and integrity. The leaders who truly stand out are those who see people as partners, view ethics as their guiding strength, and recognize trust as their greatest treasure. These are the leaders who will build workplaces where truth continues to shine brighter than fear, where empathy leads over ego, and where humanity takes precedence over hierarchy.

As this journey comes to an end, it's important to remember that leadership isn't just a title—*it's a special privilege.* Every decision a leader makes, whether noticed or not, has a ripple effect on the culture, the company, and the community. A truly ethical leader aims not only to build successful organizations but also to create a moral legacy that endures beyond profit margins and public titles.

Leadership, at its very best, is a daily choice to do good and to do it with excellence.

Bibliography

1. Allen, James Lane. The Kentucky Cardinal. Harper & Brothers, 1894.

2. Angelou, Maya. Wouldn't Take Nothing for My Journey Now. Random House, 1993.

3. Arendt, Hannah. Eichmann in Jerusalem: A Report on the Banality of Evil. Viking Press, 1963.

4. Arendt, Hannah. Responsibility and Judgment. Schocken Books, 2003.

5. Buffett, Warren. The Essays of Warren Buffett: Lessons for Corporate America. Edited by Lawrence A. Cunningham, Carolina Academic Press, 2013.

6. Buffett, Warren. The Snowball: Warren Buffett and the Business of Life. Bantam, 2008.

7. Covey, Stephen R. The 7 Habits of Highly Effective People. Simon & Schuster, 1989.

8. Dhawan, Erica. Digital Body Language: How to Build Trust and Connection, No Matter the Distance. St. Martin's Press, 2021.

9. Drucker, Peter F. Management: Tasks, Responsibilities, Practices. Harper & Row, 1974.

10. Drucker, Peter F. and Maciariello. The Daily Drucker. Harper Business, 2004.

11. Edmondson, Amy C. The Fearless Organization: Creating Psychological Safety in the Workplace for Learning, Innovation, and Growth. Wiley, 2019.

12. Einstein, Albert. The World as I See It. Philosophical Library, 1934.

13. Frankl, Viktor E. Man's Search for Meaning. Beacon Press, 1959.

14. Goleman, Daniel. Emotional Intelligence: Why It Can Matter More Than IQ. Bantam Books, 1995.

15. Huffington, Arianna. Thrive: The Third Metric to Redefining Success and Creating a Life of Well-Being, Wisdom, and Wonder. Harmony, 2014.

16. Lencioni, Patrick. The Five Dysfunctions of a Team. Jossey-Bass, 2002.

17. Mandela, Nelson. Long Walk to Freedom. Little, Brown and Company, 1994.

18. Maxwell, John C. The 21 Irrefutable Laws of Leadership. HarperCollins Leadership, 1998.

19. Myers, Vernā. What If I Say the Wrong Thing? 25 Habits for Culturally Effective People. ABA Publishing, 2013.

20. Nadella, Satya. Hit Refresh: The Quest to Rediscover Microsoft's Soul and Imagine a Better Future for Everyone. Harper Business, 2017.

21. Paine, Thomas. The American Crisis. 1776.

22. Pink, Daniel H. Drive: The Surprising Truth About What Motivates Us. Riverhead Books, 2009.

23. Schweitzer, Albert. Out of My Life and Thought. Johns Hopkins University Press, 1949.

24. Schweitzer, Albert. Reverence for Life. Peter Smith, 1998.

25. Schweitzer, Albert. The Philosophy of Civilization. Prometheus Books, 1987.

26. Shaw, George Bernard. Selected Speeches and Writings. Penguin Classics, 1996.

27. Sinek, Simon. Leaders Eat Last: Why Some Teams Pull Together and Others Don't. Portfolio, 2014.

28. Sinek, Simon. Start with Why: How Great Leaders Inspire Everyone to Take Action. Portfolio, 2009.

29. Thoreau, Henry David. Walden. Ticknor and Fields, 1854.

30. Wooden, John. Wooden on Leadership. McGraw-Hill, 2005.

www.ingramcontent.com/pod-product-compliance
Lightning Source LLC
Chambersburg PA
CBHW071154200326
41519CB00018B/5221